AF604829

I grew up near the beach in Northern New South Wales. There is plenty of bushland, high mountains and big rivers here. This land sits within the Bundjalung Nation. I am a visitor on this country as my family is from the Wiradjuri Nation. The Wiradjuri people are from South West New South Wales.

Even though my Aboriginal ancestors lived inland from the coast, that has not stopped me loving the water. I feel like the ocean is very important. The Wiradjuri Nation is not on the coastline, but it contains many rivers and lakes. Maybe that's why I like the water so much.

Growing up, I had many friends who lived near me. We all lived close to the beach and we could easily ride there with our bikes and skateboards. We carried our surfboards under our arm. My dog often came to the beach with us.

EX

After school and on the weekend, we went to the beach. It was definitely our favourite place. The winter was not too cold, and the water temperature was always warm enough to swim and surf. Sometimes we started surfing before the sun came up, and sometimes we finished surfing after the sun went down.

I loved the beach and the creek. I would fish and hunt for crabs at the creek. When I caught fish, I would share them with my friends. Sharing is very important in my culture and we always share with our family and friends.

In the afternoon after school, we would ride our bikes to the beach and watch the surf. We would work out where the best waves were breaking. We paddled out together to be safe. We would laugh and have lots of fun.

One day, we surfed until the sun went down and the light started to fade. The water was becoming dark and it was getting quite scary. The other surfers had gone back to the beach. We decided to paddle back as well. We rode our bikes home before it became too dark.

We saw many dolphins. Dolphins like to surf the waves as well and sometimes they would surf a wave with me. We also saw lots of whales and sometimes, some giant rays. I feel connected to the ocean and animals. I also like to be connected to the land. I thank the creator for these wonderful things.

Many visitors from the city would come to my hometown for holidays. One day when I was at the beach, some children became caught in a strong rip current. They were very scared and crying. I was a very strong swimmer and I went into the surf and saved them. Their parents were very grateful and thanked me.

Along the coast, there were many big sand dunes. In these dunes, you could find bush tucker and I was able to find lots of food to eat. We ate the leaves of small plants. There were also mussels on the rocks and fish in the ocean. There was lots of food if you looked closely. However, you had to know what was safe, otherwise, you could get poisoned. My Aboriginal Uncles showed me what was safe to eat.

After a big day of surfing, I always rode home to my family. My family is very large. We had brothers, sisters, cousins, nephews, and nieces all living with us. We had a big house with many rooms. Family is very important in my culture. We all stay together and support one another to have good lives. I love spending time relaxing with my family.

Word bank

Northern
mountains
Bundjalung
Nation
visitor
Wiradjuri
Aboriginal
ancestors
important
coastline
skateboards
surfboards
definitely
favourite
temperature
breaking
paddled
becoming
decided
dolphins
connected
creator
wonderful
hometown
grateful
mussels
ocean
otherwise
poisoned
cousins
nephews
nieces
relaxing